ENGLISH SUITE

for guitar solo

by JOHN W. DUARTE

This work has been recorded
by Andres Segovia on Decca Records

NOVELLO

To Andres Segovia and his wife on the occasion of their marriage

ENGLISH SUITE
for Guitar Solo
by
JOHN W. DUARTE
Opus 31

1 Prelude

19604

3

4

2 Folk Song

5

6

un poco mesto

poco rit.

étouffée _____

molto rit.

H.7

19604

3 Round Dance

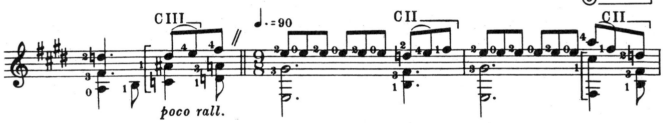

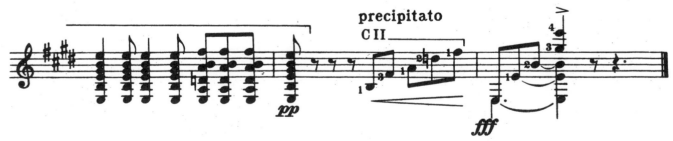